On Being Different

ON
BEING
DIFFERENT

*What It Means
To Be a Homosexual*

M E R L E   M I L L E R

RANDOM HOUSE
New York

ISBN: 0-394-47330-2
Library of Congress Catalog Card Number: 70-162391

A large part of this book first appeared in the January 17, 1971,
edition of *The New York Times Magazine* as an article entitled
"What It Means to Be a Homosexual."

Manufactured in the United States of America

24689753

First Edition

Acknowledgments

I am grateful to Victor Navasky and to Gerald Walker, editors, writers, and friends. To Victor, whose idea it really was, and to Gerry, because his telling me about *Maurice* started the writing. And to *The New York Times;* we are both the better for its having first appeared there.

M.M.

For David

What It Means
To Be a Homosexual

Eᴅ ᴡ ᴀ ʀ ᴅ Morgan Forster was a very good writer and a very gutsy man. In the essay "What I Believe," he said:

> I hate the idea of causes, and if I had to choose between betraying my country and betraying my friend, I hope I would have the guts to betray my country. Such a choice may scandalize the modern reader, and he may stretch out his patriotic hand to the telephone at once and ring up the police. It would not have shocked Dante, though. Dante places Brutus and Cassius in the lowest circle of Hell because they had chosen to betray their friend Julius Caesar rather than their country Rome.

It took courage to write those words, just as it does, at times, for anyone else to repeat them. In the early 1950s, when I wanted to use them on the title page of a book on blacklisting in television that I wrote for the American Civil Liberties Union, officials of the A.C.L.U. advised against it. Why ask for more trouble, they said. Being against blacklisting was trouble enough. Those were timorous days. "What I Believe" was included in a book of essays used in secondary schools, but it disappeared from the book around 1954 and was replaced by something or other from the *Reader's Digest*. When I protested to the publisher, he said—it was a folk saying of the time— "You have to roll with the tide." The tide was McCarthyism, which had not then fully subsided— assuming it ever has or will.

Forster was not a man who rolled with the tide. I met him twice, heard him lecture several times, was acquainted with several of his friends, and knew that he was homosexual, but I did not know that he had written a novel, *Maurice,* dealing with homosexual characters, until it was announced last November. On top of the manuscript he wrote: "Publishable— but is it worth it?" The novel, completed in 1915, will, after fifty-five years and the death of Forster, at last be published.

Is it worth it? Even so outspoken a man as Forster had to ask himself that question. It is one thing to confess to political unorthodoxy but quite another to admit to sexual unorthodoxy. Still. Yet. A homosexual friend of mine has said, "Straights don't want to know for sure, and they can never forgive you for telling them. They prefer to think it doesn't exist, but if it does, at least keep quiet about it." And one Joseph Epstein said in *Harper's* in September, 1970:

> . . . however wide the public tolerance for it, it is no more acceptable privately than it ever was . . . private acceptance of homosexuality, in my experience, is not to be found, even among the most liberal-minded, sophisticated, and liberated people. . . . Nobody says, or at least I have never heard anyone say, "Some of my best friends are homosexual." People do say—I say—"fag" and "queer" without hesitation—and these words, no matter who is uttering them, are put-down words, in intent every bit as vicious as "kike" or "nigger."

Is it true? Is that the way it is? Have my heterosexual friends, people I thought were my heterosexual friends, been going through an elaborate charade all these years? I would like to think they agree with George Weinberg, a therapist and author of a book on therapy called *The Action Approach,* who says, "I would never consider a person healthy unless he had overcome his prejudice against homosexuality." But even Mr. Weinberg assumes that there is a prejudice, apparently built-in, a natural part of the human psyche. And so my heterosexual friends had it, maybe still have it? The late Otto Kahn, I think it was, said, "A kike is a Jewish gentleman who has just left the room." Is a fag a homosexual gentleman who has just stepped out? Me?

I can never be sure, of course, will never be sure. I know it shouldn't bother me. That's what everybody says, but it does bother me. It bothers me every time I enter a room in which there is anyone else. Friend or foe? Is there a difference?

When I was a child in Marshalltown, Iowa, I hated Christmas almost as much as I do now, but I loved Halloween. I never wanted to take off the mask; I wanted to wear it everywhere, night and day, always. And I suppose I still do. I have often used liquor, which is another kind of mask, and, more recently, pot.

Then, too, I suppose if my friends have been playing games with me, they might with justice say that I have been playing games with them. It took me almost fifty years to come out of the closet, to stop pretending to be something I was not, most of the time fooling nobody.

But I guess it is never easy to open the closet door. When she talked to the Daughters of Bilitis, a Les-

bian organization, late in the summer of 1970, Kate
Millett, author of *Sexual Politics,* said, "I'm very
glad to be here. It's been kind of a long trip. . . . I've
wanted to be here, I suppose, in a surreptitious way
for a long time, and I was always too chicken. . . .
Anyway, I'm out of the closet. Here I am."

Not surprisingly, Miss Millett is now being attacked
more because of what she said to the Daughters of
Bilitis than because of what she said in her book.
James Owles, president of Gay Activists' Alliance, a
militant, nonviolent organization concerned with civil
rights for homosexuals, says, "We don't give a damn
whether people like us or not. We want the rights
we're entitled to."

I'm afraid I want both. I dislike being despised,
unless I have done something despicable, realizing
that the simple fact of being homosexual is all by
itself despicable to many people, maybe, as Mr.
Epstein says, to everybody who is straight. Assuming
anybody is ever totally one thing sexually.

Mr. Epstein says, "When it comes to homosexuality, we know, or ought to know, that we know
next to nothing"—and that seems to me to be true.
Our ignorance of the subject is almost as great now
as it was in 1915 when Forster wrote *Maurice*—

almost as great as it was in 1815 or, for that matter,
1715. Freud did not add much knowledge to the subject, nor have any of his disciples, none that I have
read or listened to, none that I have consulted. I have
spent several thousand dollars and several thousand
hours with various practitioners, and while they have
often been helpful in leading me to an understanding
of how I got to be the way I am, none of them has
ever had any feasible, to me feasible, suggestion as to
how I could be any different.

And that includes the late Dr. Edmund Bergler,
who claimed not only that he could "cure" me but
get rid of my writer's block as well. He did neither.
I am still homosexual, and I have a writer's block
every morning when I sit down at the typewriter.
And it's too late now to change my nature. At fifty,
give or take a year or so, I am afraid I will have to
make do with me. Which is what my mother said in
the beginning.

Nobody seems to know why homosexuality happens, how it happens, or even what it is that does
happen. Assuming *it* happens in any one way. Or
any thousand ways. We do not even know how prevalent it is. We were told in 1948 by Dr. Alfred C.

Kinsey in *Sexual Behavior in the Human Male* that thirty-seven percent of all males have had or will have at least one homosexual experience between adolescence and old age. And last year a questionnaire answered by some twenty thousand readers of *Psychology Today* brought the same response. Thirty-seven percent of the males said that they had had one homosexual experience. (I will be speaking in what follows largely of male homosexuality, which has been my experience.)

Voltaire is said to have had one such experience, with an Englishman. When the Englishman suggested that they repeat it, Voltaire is alleged to have said, "If you try it once, you are a philosopher; if twice, you are a sodomite."

The National Institute of Mental Health says that between three and four million Americans of both sexes are predominantly homosexual, while many others display what the institute delicately calls occasional homosexual tendencies.

But how do they know? Because the closets are far from emptied; there are more in hiding than out of hiding. That has been my experience anyway. And homosexuals come in all shapes and sizes, sometimes in places where you'd least expect to find them. If Jim

9

Bouton is to be believed, in big league baseball and, if we are to go along with Dave Meggysey, in the National Football League. Nobody knows. The question as to who is and who isn't was not asked in the 1970 census.

A Harris survey indicates that sixty-three percent of the American people feel that homosexuals are "harmful" to American society. One wonders—I wondered anyway—how those thirty-seven percent of the males with one admitted homosexual experience responded to the question. After how many such experiences does one get to be harmful? And harmful in what way? The inquisitive Mr. Harris appears not to have asked. Harmful. Feared. Hated. What do the hardhats find objectionable in the young? Their lack of patriotism and the fact that they are all faggots. Aren't they? We're in the midst of a "freaking fag revolution," said the prosecutor in the Chicago conspiracy trial. At least that seems to be the politically profitable thing to say in Chicago.

In the 1950s, McCarthy found that attacking homosexuals paid off almost as well as attacking the Communists, and he claimed they were often the same. Indeed, the District of Columbia police set up a special detail of the vice squad "to investigate links between homosexuality and Communism."

On Being Different

The American Civil Liberties Union recently has been commendably active in homosexual cases, but in the early fifties, when homosexuals and people accused of homosexuality were being fired from all kinds of Government posts, as they still are, the A.C.L.U. was notably silent. And the most silent of all was a closet queen who was a member of the board of directors, myself.

Epstein, a proclaimed liberal, said in *Harper's*:

If a close friend were to reveal himself to me as being a homosexual, I am very uncertain what my reaction would be—except to say that it would not be simple. . . . If I had the power to do so, I would wish homosexuality off the face of this earth.

I could not help wondering what Epstein, who is, I believe, a literary critic, would do about the person and the work of W. H. Auden, homosexual and generally considered to be the greatest living poet in English. "We must love one another or die." Except for homosexuals?

> *Beleaguered by the same*
> *Negation and despair,*
> *Show an affirming flame.*

The great fear is that a son will turn out to be homosexual. Nobody seems to worry about a Lesbian daughter; nobody talks about it anyway. But the former runs through every level of our culture. In the song Peggy Lee recently made popular, "Love Story," part of the lyric has to do with the son she and her husband will have, *He's got to be straight/We don't want a bent one.* In the Arpège ad this Christmas: "Promises, husbands to wives, 'I promise to stop telling you that our youngest is developing effeminate tendencies.'"

And so on, and on. I should add that not all mothers are afraid that their sons will be homosexuals. Everywhere among us are those dominant ladies who welcome homosexuality in their sons. That way the mothers know they won't lose them to another woman.

And, of course, no television writer would feel safe without at least one fag joke per script. Carson, Cavett, and Griffin all give their audiences the same knowing grin when *that* subject is mentioned, and audiences always laugh, though somewhat nervously.

Is homosexuality contagious? Once again, nobody seems to know for sure. The writer Richard Rhodes reports that those tireless and tedious investigators Dr. William Masters and Mrs. Virginia Johnson of

St. Louis have got into the subject of homosexuality. And Masters *hinted* to Rhodes that his clinical work had shown that "homosexual seduction in adolescence is generally the predetermining factor in later homosexual choice."

One should not hold the indefatigable doctor to a "hint," but the Wolfenden Committee set up by the British Government in the fifties to study homosexuality and prostitution found the opposite:

It is a view widely held, and one which found favor among our police and legal witnesses, that seduction in youth is the decisive factor in the production of homosexuality as a condition, and we are aware that this condition has done much to alarm parents and teachers. We have found no convincing evidence in support of this contention. Our medical witnesses unanimously held that seduction has little effect in inducing a settled pattern of homosexual behavior, and we have been given no grounds from other sources which contradict their judgment. Moreover, it has been suggested to us that the fact of being seduced often does less harm to the victim than the publicity which attends the criminal proceedings against the offender and the distress which undue alarm sometimes leads parents to show.

Martin Hoffman, a San Francisco psychiatrist who has written a book about male homosexuality called *The Gay World,* said in a recent issue of *Psychology Today*:

> Until we know about the mechanisms of sexual arousal in the central nervous system and how learning factors can set the triggering devices for those mechanisms, we cannot have a satisfactory theory of homosexual behavior. We must point out that heterosexual behavior is as much of a scientific puzzle as homosexual behavior. . . . We assume that heterosexual arousal is somehow natural and needs no explanation. I suggest that to call it natural is to evade the whole issue; it is as if we said it's natural for the sun to come up in the morning and left it at that. Is it possible that we know less about human sexuality than the medieval astrologers knew about the stars?

I know this. Almost the first words I remember hearing, maybe the first words I choose to remember hearing, were my mother's, saying, "We ordered a little girl, and when you came along, we were somewhat disappointed." She always claimed that I came from Montgomery Ward, and when I would point out that there was no baby department in the Monkey Ward catalogue, she would say, "This was special."

I never knew what that meant, but I never asked. I knew enough. I knew that I was a disappointment. "But we love you just the same," my mother would say, "and we'll have to make do."

We had to make do with a great many things in those days. The Depression came early to our house, around 1927, when my father lost all his money in the Florida land boom, and once we got poor, we stayed poor. "You'll have the wing for supper, because this is a great big chicken and will last for days, and tomorrow you can take a whole leg to school in your little lunch pail and have it all to yourself." Day-old bread, hand-me-down clothes that had once belonged to more prosperous cousins, holes in the soles of my shoes—all of it. I was a combination of Oliver Twist and Little Nell.

They say that the Depression and the World War were the two central experiences of my generation, and that may be. I certainly had more than enough of both, but I was never really hungry for food. It was love I craved, approval, forgiveness for being what I could not help being. And I have spent a good part of my life looking for those things, always, as a few psychologists have pointed out, in the places I was least likely to find them.

My baby blankets were all pink, purchased before

the disaster, my birth. The lace on my baby dress was pink; my bonnet was fringed with pink, and little old ladies were forever peering into the baby buggy and crib, saying, "What an adorable little girl." They kept on saying that until I got my first butch haircut, at four, just before I started kindergarten. Until then I had long, straight hair, mouse-brown, lusterless, and long hair was just as unpopular in Marshalltown then as it is now.

Not until college did I read that Oscar Wilde's mother started him down the garden path by letting his hair grow and dressing him as a little girl. As Oscar said, "Children begin by loving their parents; as they grow older they judge them; sometimes they forgive them."

I was four years old when I started school. My mother had told them I was five; I was somewhat precocious, and she may just have wanted to get me out of the house. But butch haircut or not, some boys in the third grade took one look at me and said, "Hey, look at the sissy," and they started laughing. It seems to me now that I heard that word at least once five days a week for the next thirteen years, until I skipped town and went to the university. Sissy and all the other words—pansy, fairy, nance, fruit, fruitcake, and less printable epithets. I did not encounter the word faggot until I got to Manhattan. I'll tell you this, though. It's not true, that saying about sticks and stones; it's words that break your bones.

They used to call my friend Sam G. a kike, but that was behind his back. The black boy and black girl in my high school class were "jigs" or "coons," but that, too, was behind their backs. Some Catholic boys were "mackerel snappers," but to their faces only if they were much younger and weaker.

I was the only one they looked right at when they said the damning words, and the only thing I can think of to my credit is the fact that I almost never ran away; I almost always stared them down; I almost never cried until later, when I was alone.

I admit I must have been a splendid target, under-sized always, the girlish voice, the steel-rimmed glasses, always bent, no doubt limp of wrist, and I habitually carried a music roll. I studied both piano and violin all through school, and that all by itself was enough to condemn one to permanent *sissydom*.

When I was doing a television documentary of Harry Truman's life, he said at one point, "I was never what you'd call popular when I went to school. The popular boys were the athletes with their big, tight fists, and I was never like that. . . . I always had a music roll and wore thick glasses; I was wall-eyed, you know. . . . I stopped playing the piano when I was fourteen years old. Where I come from, playing the piano wasn't considered the proper thing for a boy to do."

I said, "Mr. President, did they ever call you 'four-eyes' when you were a little boy?"

"Oh, yes," he said, " 'four-eyes,' 'sissy,' and a lot of other things. When that happens, what you have to do is, you have to work harder than they do and be smarter, and if you are, things usually turn out all right in the end."

As a child I wanted to be the girl my mother had had in mind—or else the All-American boy everybody else so admired. Since sex changes were unheard of in those days, I clearly couldn't be a girl; so I tried the other. I ate carloads of Wheaties, hoping I'd turn into another Jack Armstrong, but I still could neither throw nor catch a baseball. I couldn't even see the thing; I'd worn glasses as thick as plate-glass windows since I was three. ("You inherited your father's eyes, among other weaknesses:") I sold enough *Liberty* magazines to buy all the body-building equipment Charles Atlas had to offer, but it did no good. I remained an eighty-nine-pound weakling year after year. And when the voices of all the other boys in my class had changed into a very low baritone, I was still an uncertain soprano, and remained that until I got to the University of Iowa in Iowa City and, among other disguises, lowered my voice at least two octaves so that I could get a job as a radio announcer on the university station.

I also became city editor of *The Daily Iowan* and modeled myself after a character out of *The Front Page*, wearing a hat indoors and out, talking out of the corner of my mouth, never without a cigarette, being folksy with the local cops, whom I detested, one and all. I chased girls, never with much enthusiasm I'm afraid, and denounced queers—I hadn't yet come on the word fag—with some regularity in the column I wrote for the *Iowan*. Most of those odd people were in the university theater, or so I chose to pretend, and while I never came right out and said they were sexually peculiar, I hinted at it. They wore what was by the standards of the time long hair, and I denounced that as well. What a fink I was—anything to avoid being called a sissy again.

I was afraid I would never get into the army, but

after the psychiatrist tapped me on the knee with a little hammer and asked how I felt about girls, before I really had a chance to answer, he said, "Next," and I was being sworn in. For the next four years as an editor of *Yank*, first in the Pacific and then in Europe, I continued to use my deepest city-editor's–radio-announcer's voice, ordered reporters and photographers around and kept my evenings to myself, especially in Paris.

After the war, I became as much a part of the Establishment as I had ever been, including servitude as an editor of *Time*. I remember in particular a long discussion about whether to use the picture of a British composer on the cover because a researcher had discovered that he was . . . I am sure if there was a vote, I voted against using the picture.

A little later, after finishing my first successful novel, *That Winter*, which became a best seller, I decided there was no reason at all why I couldn't be just as straight as the next man. I might not be able to play baseball, but I could get married.

Peter Ilyich Tchaikovsky had the same idea. Maybe marriage would cure him of what he called "The." But, afterwards, in a letter to his friend Nadejda von Meck, he wrote:

. . . I saw right away that I could never love my wife and that the *habit* on which I had counted would never come. I fell into despair and longed for death. . . . My mind began to go. . . .

Peter Ilyich's marriage lasted only two weeks. My own lasted longer and was not quite so searing an experience, but it could not have succeeded.

Lucy Komisar says in *Washington Monthly* that this country is obsessed by what she calls "violence and the masculine mystique," which is certainly true enough. "The enemies of national 'virility' are called 'effete,' a word that means 'sterile, spent, worn-out,' and conjures up the picture of an effeminate pantywaist." Also true, but Americans are certainly not the first people to get uptight about "virility."

Philip of Macedon was forever fussing at Olympias because he claimed she was making their son Alexander effeminate. And, to be sure, Alexander turned out to be at least bisexual, maybe totally homosexual. How else could one explain his grief at the death of his lover, Hephaestion? According to Plutarch:

Alexander was so beyond all reason transported that, to express his sorrow, he immediately ordered the manes and tails of all his horses and mules cut, and threw down the battlements of the neighboring cities. The poor physician he crucified, and forbade playing on the flute or any other musical instrument in the camp a great while. . . .

Gore Vidal has been quoted as saying, "The Italians are sexual opportunists. Anything that feels good, they're for it." Which may be true, but I cannot imagine an Italian father who would not be devastated if he found that his son was homosexual. Or, for that matter, a father in any country in Western society. In England, where the Sexual Offenses Act has been on the law books since 1967, ten years after the recommendations of the Wolfenden Committee, Anthony Gray, director of an organization that helps sexual minorities, says that even today ". . . the briefest experience is enough to convince one that discrimination against known homosexuals is still the rule rather than the exception." Gray notes that homosexuals still cannot belong to the Civil Service and are still likely to lose their jobs if "found out."

Most members of the Gay Liberation Front appear to believe that Marxism is the answer, which is odd because in Communist China homosexuals are put in prisons for brainwashing that are called "hospitals for ideological reform." Chairman Mao has said, "Our object in exposing errors and criticizing short-comings is like that of a doctor in curing a disease." In Cuba homosexuals have been placed in concentration camps.

Still, as Huey P. Newton, Supreme Commander of the Black Panther Party, has said, there is no reason to think a homosexual cannot be a revolutionary. In late summer of 1970, shortly after the New York chapter of the Gay Liberation Front gave a $500 donation to the Panthers, Newton, in a rambling, rather tortured statement said, "What made them homosexuals? Some people say that it's the decadence of capitalism. I don't know whether this is the case; I rather doubt it. . . . But there's nothing to say that a homosexual cannot also be a revolutionary. . . . Quite the contrary, maybe a homosexual could be the most revolutionary."

On the other hand, Eldridge Cleaver in *Soul on Ice* gives what I am sure is a more prevalent view among the Panthers: "Homosexuality is a sickness, just as are baby-rape or wanting to become head of General Motors."

Of course, the Soviet Union claims not to have any homosexuals. I cannot comment on the validity of that claim, never having been there, but I do know that when one of the Russian ballet companies is in town, you can hear a great many Russian accents on West 42d Street and in various gay bars.

Growing up in Marshalltown, I was allowed to take as many books as I wanted from the local library, and I always wanted as many as I could carry, eight or ten at a time. I read about sensitive boys, odd boys, boys who were lonely and misunderstood, boys who really didn't care all that much for baseball, boys who were teased by their classmates, books about all of these, but for years nobody in any of the books I read was ever tortured by the strange fantasies that tore at me every time, for instance, my mother insisted I go to the "Y" to learn how to swim. They swam nude at the "Y," and I never went. Lead me not into temptation. In gym—it was required in high school—I always tried to get in and out of the locker room before anybody else arrived.

And in none of the books I read did anybody feel a compulsion, and compulsion it surely was, to spend so many hours, almost as many as I spent at the library, in or near the Minneapolis & St. Louis railroad station, where odd, frightening things were written on the walls of the men's room. And where in those days, there were always boys in their teens and early twenties who were on their way to and from somewhere in freight cars. Boys who were hungry and jobless and who for a very small amount of money, and sometimes none at all, were available for sex; almost always they were. They needed the money, and they needed someone to recognize them, to actually see them.

That was the way it happened the first time. The boy was from Chicago, and his name was Carl. He was seventeen, and I was twelve and the aggressor. I remember every detail of it; I suppose one always does. Carl hadn't eaten, said he hadn't eaten for two days. His father was a plumber, unemployed, and his mother was, he said rather vaguely, "away, hopefully forever." I remember once I said, "But why don't you go home anyway?" And he said, "Where would that be?"

Years later a boy I met on West 42d Street said it best, about the boys in my childhood and the boys on all the streets of all the cities where they wait. He was the next-to-youngest child in a very poor family of nine, and once he ran away from home for two days and two nights, and when he got back, nobody knew that he had been gone. Then, at nineteen, he discovered The Street, and he said, "All of a sudden here were all these men, and they were looking at me."

The boys who stopped by at the M. and St. L. in Marshalltown all had stories, and they were all anxious to tell them. They were all lonely and afraid. None of them ever made fun of me. I was never beaten up. They recognized, I guess, that we were fellow aliens with no place to register.

Like my three friends in town. They were aliens, too: Sam, whose father ran a grocery store my mother wouldn't patronize. ("Always buy American, Merle, and don't you forget it. We don't know *where* the Jews send the money you spend in one of their stores.") A girl in a wheelchair, a polio victim; we talked through every recess in school. And there was the woman with a clubfoot who sold tickets at the Casino, a movie house, and let me in for free—tickets couldn't have been a dime then, but they were—until I was sixteen, and, as I say, skipped town.

The black boy and the black girl in my high school class never spoke to me, and I never spoke to them. That was the way it was. It never occurred to me that that was not necessarily the way it was meant to be.

There were often black boys on the freight trains,

and we talked and had sex. Their stories were always sadder than anybody else's. I never had any hangups about the color of somebody's skin. If you were an outcast, that was good enough for me. I once belonged to twenty-two organizations devoted to improving the lot of the world's outcasts. The only group of outcasts I never spoke up for publicly, never donated money to or signed an ad or petition for were the homosexuals. I always used my radio announcer's voice when I said "No."

I was fourteen when I happened on a book called *Winesburg, Ohio.* I don't know how. Maybe it was recommended by the librarian, a kind and knowing woman with the happy name of Alice Story. Anyway, there at last, in a story called "Hands," were the words I had been looking for. I was not the only sissy in the world:

> Adolf Myers was meant to be a teacher . . . In their feeling for the boys under their charge such men are not unlike the finer sort of women in their love of men.

Sherwood Anderson's story ended unhappily. Of course. How else could it end?

And then the tragedy. A half-witted boy of the school becomes enamored of the young master. In his bed at night he imagined unthinkable things and in the morning went forth to tell his dreams as facts. Strange, hideous accusations fell from his loose-hung lips. Through the Pennsylvania town went a shiver. Hidden, shadowy doubts that had been in men's minds concerning Adolf Myers were galvanized into beliefs.

I must have read "Hands" more than any story before or since. I can still quote it from beginning to end:

They had intended to hang the schoolmaster, but something in his figure, so small, white, and piti-ful, touched their hearts and they let him escape.

Naturally. If you were *that way*, what else could you expect? Either they ran you out of town or you left before they got around to it. I decided on the latter. I once wrote that I started packing to leave Marshalltown when I was two years old, which is a slight exaggeration.

As he ran into the darkness, they repented of their weakness and ran after him, swearing and throwing sticks and great balls of soft mud at the figure that screamed and ran faster into the darkness.

Winesburg was published in 1919, and one of the terrifying things is that the people in any town in the United States, quite likely any city, too, would react very much the same way today, wouldn't they?

Look what happened only fifteen years ago, in 1955, in Boise, Idaho, when a "homosexual underworld" was uncovered. The "upright" citizens panicked, and some people left town, some were run out of town, and others were sentenced to long prison terms.

In a perceptive and thorough account of what happened, *The Boys of Boise,* John Gerassi reports that a lawyer told him that during the height of the hysteria the old American custom of a night on the town with the boys disappeared entirely:

> You never saw so many men going out to the bars at night with their wives and girl friends . . . we used to have a poker game once a week. Well, for a few weeks we canceled them. Then one of the guys got an idea: "We'll invite a girl to play with us. You know, it's not very pleasant to play poker with women, not when you're in a serious game. But that's what we had to do."

I have been back to Marshalltown only briefly in all the years since my escape, but a few years ago I did return to a reunion of my high school class. I made the principal speech at the banquet, and at the end there was enough applause to satisfy my ego temporarily, and various of my classmates, all of whom looked depressingly middle-aged, said various pleasant things, after which there was a dance.

I have written about that before, but what I have not written about, since I was still not ready to come out of the closet, is that a little while after the dance began, a man whose face had been only vaguely familiar and whose name I would not have remembered if he had not earlier reminded me came up, an idiot grin on his face, his wrists limp, his voice falsetto, and said, "How about letting me have this dance, sweetie?" He said it loud enough for all to hear.

I said, "I'm terribly sorry, but my dance card is all filled up." By no means the wittiest of remarks, but under the circumstances it was the best I could manage.

Later, several people apologized for what he had said, but I wondered (who would not?) how many of them had been tempted to say the same thing. Or would say something of the kind after I had gone.

Fag, faggot, sissy, queer. A fag is a homosexual gentleman who has just left the room.

And the man who said it was a successful newspaper executive in Colorado, in his mid-forties, a father of five, I was told, a grandfather. After all those years, twenty-seven of them, was he still . . . what? Threatened by me? Offended? Unsettled? Challenged? No children or grandchildren around to be perverted. Was his own sexual identity so shaky that . . .? A closet queen at heart? No, that's too easy. And it's too easy to say that he's the one who needs treatment, not me. George Weinberg says:

> The "homosexual problem," as I have described it here, is the problem of condemning *variety* in human existence. If one cannot enjoy the fact of this variety, at the very least one must learn to become indifferent to it, since obviously it is here to stay.

The fear of it simply will not go away, though. A man who was once a friend, maybe my best friend, the survivor of five marriages, the father of nine, not too long ago told me that his eldest son was coming to my house on Saturday: "Now, please try not to make a pass at him."

He laughed. I guess he meant it as a joke; I didn't ask.

And a man I've known, been acquainted with, let's say, for twenty-five years, called from the city on a Friday afternoon before getting on the train to come up to my place for the weekend. He said, "I've always leveled with you, Merle, and I'm going to now. I've changed my mind about bringing —— [his sixteen-year-old son]. I'm sure you understand.

I said that, no, I didn't understand. Perhaps he could explain it to me.

He said, "—— is only an impressionable kid, and while I've known you and know you wouldn't, but suppose you had some friends in, and . . .?"

I suggested that he not come for the weekend. I have never molested a child my whole life through, never seduced anybody, assuming that word has meaning, and, so far as I know, neither have any of my homosexual friends. Certainly not in my living room or bedroom. Moreover, I have known quite a few homosexuals, and I have listened to a great many accounts of how they got that way or think they got that way. I have never heard anybody say that he (or she) got to be homosexual because of seduction.

But, then, maybe it is contagious, floating in the

air around me, like a virus. Homosexuals themselves often seem to think so. How else can you explain the self-pitying *The Boys in the Band*?

Martin Hoffman, the San Francisco therapist I mentioned earlier, says:

> Self-condemnation pervades the homosexual world and, in concert with the psychodynamic and bio-logical factors that lead toward promiscuity, makes stable relationships a terrific problem. In spite of the fact that so many homosexuals are lonely and alone, they can't seem to find someone with whom to share even part of their lives. This dilemma is the core problem of the gay world and stems in large measure from the adverse self-definitions that society imprints on the homosexual mind. Until we can change these ancient attitudes, many men— including some of our own brothers, sons, friends, colleagues and children yet unborn—will live out their lives in the quiet desperation of the sad gay world.

Perhaps. None of my homosexual friends are any too happy, but then very few of my heterosexual friends—supposed friends, I should say—are exactly joyous, either. And as for the promiscuity and short-

33

term relationships, neither of those has been quite true in my case, and only recently I attended an anniversary party of two homosexuals who had been together for twenty-five years, reasonably constant, reasonably happy. They still hold hands, though not in public, and they are kind to each other, which is rare enough anywhere these days.

Late in October, 1970, members of the Gay Activists Alliance staged an all-day sit-in at *Harper's* to protest the Epstein article, surely the first time in the 120-year history of the magazine that that has happened. And as Peter Fisher, a student at Columbia who helped organize the sit-in, kept saying, "What you don't understand is that there's been a revolution."

I'm not sure it's a full-scale revolution yet, but there's been a revolt, and for thousands of young homosexuals, and some not so young, the quiet desperation that Hoffman talks about is all over. They are neither quiet nor desperate.

The whole thing began with an event that has been compared to the Boston Tea Party or the firing on Fort Sumter: the Stonewall Rebellion. On June 28, 1969, the police started to raid a gay bar in the

West Village, the Stonewall Inn. The police are forever raiding gay bars, especially around election time,
when they also move in on West 42d Street. And in
the past, what you did was, you took the cops' abuse,
and sometimes you went off with only a few familiar
epithets or a hit on the head. And sometimes you
were taken to the station on one charge or another
and, usually, released the next morning.

But that is not what happened on June 28, 1969.
A friend of mine who was there said, "It was fan-
tastic. The crowd was a fairly typical weekend crowd,
your usual queens and kids from the sticks, and the
people that are always around the bars, mostly young.
But this time instead of submitting to the cops' abuse,
the sissies fought back. They started pulling up park-
ing meters and throwing rocks and coins at the cops,
and the cops had to take refuge in the bar and call for
reinforcements. . . . It was beautiful."

That was the beginning, and on the anniversary
last summer between five thousand and fifteen thousand gay people of both sexes marched up Sixth Avenue from Sheridan Square to the Sheep Meadow in
Central Park for a "gay-in." Other, smaller parades
took place in Chicago and Los Angeles, and all three
cities survived the sight and sound of men with their

arms around men and women kissing women, chanting, "Shout it loud, gay is proud," "Three-five-seven-nine, Lesbians are mighty fine," carrying signs that said, "We Are the People Our Parents Warned Us Against," singing "We Shall Overcome."

And something else perhaps even more important happened during the 1970 elections. When Arthur J. Goldberg, running for Governor of New York, paid what was to have been a routine campaign visit to the intersection of 85th and Broadway, more than three dozen members of the G.A.A. were waiting for him. They shook his hand and asked if he was in favor of fair employment for homosexuals and of repeal of the state laws against sodomy. Goldberg's answer to each question was, "I think there are more important things to think about."

But before the election Goldberg had issued a public statement answering yes to both questions, promising as well to work against police harassment of homosexuals. The candidates for senator, Richard Ottinger and Charles Goodell, also issued statements supporting constitutional rights for homosexuals. Of course, Governor Rockefeller and Senator Buckley, the winners, remained silent on those issues, but Representative Bella Abzug, one of the earliest supporters

of G.A.A., won, and so did people like State Assem-
blyman Antonio Olivieri, the first Democrat elected
in the 66th Assembly District in fifty-five years.
Olivieri took an ad in a G.A.A. benefit program that
served to thank the organization for its support.

Marty Robinson, an extremely vocal young man, a
carpenter by profession, who was then in charge of
political affairs for G.A.A., said that "this election
serves notice on every politician in the state and
nation that homosexuals are not going to hide any
more. We're becoming militant, and we won't be
harassed or degraded any more."

John Paul Hudson, one of the alliance's found-
ers, said: "G.A.A. is a political organization. Every-
thing is done with an eye toward political effect. . . .
G.A.A. adopted this policy because all oppression of
homosexuals can only be ended by means of a power-
ful political bloc."

For an organization only a little more than a year
old and with only 180 paid-up members, G.A.A. has
certainly made itself heard. And that, according to
Arthur Evans, another fiery member, is just the
beginning. He said, "At the end of June we had a
statement that gay is good. We had a joyous celebra-
tion, as is right. But today we know not only that gay

is good, gay is angry. We are telling all the politicians and elected officials of New York State that they are going to become responsible to the people. We will make them responsible to us, or we will stop the conduct of the business of government." Well.

Small wonder that the Mattachine Society, which for twenty years has been trying to educate straight people to accept homosexuals, is now dismissed by some members of G.A.A. and the Gay Liberation Front as "the N.A.A.C.P. of our movement."

Laws discriminating against homosexuals will almost surely be changed. If not this year, in 1972; if not in 1972, in 1976; if not in 1976 . . .

Private acceptance of homosexuals and homosexuality will take somewhat longer. Most of the psychiatric establishment will continue to insist that homosexuality is a disease, and homosexuals, unlike the blacks, will not benefit from any guilt feelings on the part of liberals. So far as I can make out, there simply aren't any such feelings. On the contrary, most people of every political persuasion seem to be too uncertain of their own sexual identification to be anything but defensive. Fearful. And maybe it is contagious. Prove it isn't.

I have never infected anybody, and it's too late for

the head people to do anything about me now. Gay is good. Gay is proud. Well, yes, I suppose. If I had been given a choice (but who is?), I would prefer to have been straight. But then, would I rather not have been me? Oh, I think not, not this morning anyway. It is a very clear day in late December, and the sun is shining on the pine trees outside my studio. The air is extraordinary clear, and the sky is the color it gets only at this time of year, dark, almost navy-blue. On such a day I would not choose to be anyone else or any place else.

Afterword

May, 1971

———————◆———————

B efore I started work on the essay that appeared in *The New York Times Magazine* in January, I did not intend writing anything factual on the subject; I certainly did not intend writing so personal a piece. True, the narrator of the first-person novel on which I have been working for three years is a homosexual, but that isn't me. For one thing, his name is George Lionel, and isn't disguise one of the uses of fiction?

I have no taste for self-revelation, and I had had quite enough of crusades. I was perfectly willing to sign an occasional ad for the *Times* supporting this good cause or that. And I still considered myself a radical, more closely akin to the new left than the old, but homosexuality was not about to be my last crusade. I was not even sure it was a proper subject for a crusade.

Yes, I knew that a little more than a year before, there had been a rebellion against the cops at a gay bar named the Stonewall in Manhattan. Fine, but since moving into a glass house in the country—somebody once called it "the glass mausoleum"—I am an infrequent visitor to gay bars and was never comfortable in them.

Yes, I knew that last summer several thousand people had marched up Sixth Avenue and into Central Park for a gay-in. But my diminishing energies and enthusiasms seemed to be exhausted by once in a while making a speech or marching in a protest against the war in Southeast Asia. Gay radicalism was for the young; at my age, my principal concerns were more for my digestion than for politics—or sex.

And then the Epstein article appeared in *Harper's*, and I was both outraged and saddened. First of all, I was an alumnus of the staff of the magazine and was still a contributor, and I considered its editors friends. I also thought it was one of the best, maybe the best, magazine in the country. Yet here was a piece filled with the most blatant bigotry, the most juvenile mistakes. And with this, to me, terrifying statement: ". . . If I had the power to do so, I would wish homosexuality off the face of the earth. I would do so because I think that it brings infinitely more pain than pleasure to those who are forced to live with it."

Genocide, followed by the humanizing afterthought. Would it not be as human to wish all blacks off the face of the earth because of the pain? . . . All Jews?

Elinor Green, who was once my wife and is still my friend, was in the glass house for the Labor Day weekend; she read the piece. First, she said, she thought it was tedious, but, yes, it was also outrageous; it was harmful and hurtful, but what could one do?

I realized then that in all the years I have known Elinor, almost twenty-five, married for more than four, we had never discussed the subject of homosexuality, never mentioned that I was one. And we didn't that day or night.

I don't know what to make of that silence; I'm not proud of it, but judging from the letters I've received since the piece appeared, many of them from married men, such silence is not uncommon in American life today.

. . . I have been married for more than twenty years, have a daughter who is twenty and in college, and another who is eighteen and will start college in the fall. We have a beautiful home and, I feel, a good life together. . . . For me the thrills, excitements, and beauties of sex have always come from men. . . . I would like to open the door and have gay friends to my house and have the knowledge accepted . . . Has this ever been done successfully? If so, how? How can you change a person's mind when "homosexual" is a very dirty word, although they have lived over twenty years with one, lovingly.

The day Elinor left I called my friend of twenty-five years, Bob Kotlowitz, who was then executive editor of *Harper's*. I told Bob, who is a brave and generous man, that I thought Epstein's article was an outrage, and he said, "A great many intelligent people feel the way he does, Merle."

I said, "Do you feel that way?"

He thought for a moment, and then he said, "Oh, I suppose, more or less."

That was the time for me to have said, "After all these years, is that what you think of me?" But I didn't. The moment passed. It passed as it had passed so many hundreds of times before, so many thousands of times before.

A young homosexual friend recently said, "It's no secret that you, that one, has such-and-such color hair, is yea high, weighs thus and so, and so on, but when you keep one part of yourself secret, that becomes the most important part of you."

And that is true, I think; it may be the most important truth of all.

A few days after the talk with Kotlowitz, I had

lunch with two friends who are on the staff of *The New York Times Magazine*. I asked one of them, Victor Navasky, who is also a writer, what he thought of the Epstein piece. He said he thought it was brilliant. He said, "At a time when everybody else is saying we have to understand and accept homosexuals, Epstein is saying . . ."

I said, "Epstein is saying genocide for queers." And then for the first time, in broad daylight, before what I guess you would call a mixed audience, in a French restaurant on West 46th Street, I found myself saying, "Look, goddamn it, I'm homosexual, and most of my best friends are Jewish homosexuals, and some of my best friends are black homosexuals, and I am sick and tired of reading and hearing such goddamn demeaning, degrading bullshit about me and my friends."

There it was, out at last, and if it seems like nothing very much, I can only say that it took a long time to say it, to be able to say it, and none of the journey was easy.

If you were to ask—a great many people have—whether I regret saying it and regret what followed, I would have honestly to answer that I don't know. I may never know. Today it is raining, one of those warm, refreshing rains that I spend dispiriting winter days trying to remember. Today I don't regret it.

> . . . Though, like you, Mr. Miller, I have found an adjustment to homosexuality (with a relationship that is now in its sixth year and growing stronger and more tender daily), it is curious to speculate how much more might have been accomplished had the time spent on needless guilt and evasiveness been put to the service of self-fulfillment. The waste is one which is felt not only by myself and my lover, but by nearly every other homosexual—male or female—I have ever known.

A few days after the lunch I was at the *Times* to use the library, and Victor asked if I'd be willing to write a piece on some of the things I'd said at lunch. I said yes and immediately regretted it, which is the story of my life.

In any case, Victor called later in the week to say that after one of the longest editorial meetings in the history of the *Times Magazine,* its editors wanted me to write a piece on what he called, ". . . changing attitudes toward homosexuality, your own included . . . Make it as personal as you like . . ."

I was not, however, to proselytize; William F.

Buckley had said that he had no objection to Gore
Vidal's bisexuality; however, if Gore tried to proselytize, there was a moral issue involved . . .

I said that if there was one thing in the world that
I was not about to line up recruits for, it was homosexuality. Homosexuality and the army.

Also, Victor said, the subject was by its very nature
hazardous, but if the piece was unacceptable the
Times would still pay its usual consolation prize of
$250.

I was aware of some of the hazards so far as the
Times was concerned. Until ten, maybe five, years
before—nobody knew for sure how many—the word
"homosexual" had never even been mentioned in the
Times. Homosexual news, if any, was not considered
fit to print. In a family newspaper.

That attitude still exists, in surprising places. I
appeared on the Dick Cavett Show to discuss the subject, but when I was suggested for the David Frost
Show, I am reliably informed that I was said to be
"unacceptable." Why? The producer said, "Because
we are a family program."

I did not know at the time I was working on the
article that one of the reasons Stanley Kauffmann is
no longer dramatic critic of the *Times* had to do with

a column he had written about homosexual play-
wrights. According to Turner Catledge's book *My
Life and the* Times, the mother of Arthur Ochs
"Punch" Sulzburger was "deeply disturbed" by the
column.

I must say, on rereading it, that the column seems
remarkably mild, even for 1966:

> The homosexual dramatist ought to have the same
> freedom that the heterosexual has. While we deny
> him that freedom, we have no cause for complaint
> when he uses disguises in order to write. Further,
> to deny him that freedom is to encourage a some-
> what precious esthetics that, out of understandable
> vindictiveness, is hostile to the main stream of our
> culture. . . . It seems to me that only by such free-
> dom can our theater be freed of "homosexual
> influence"—a misnomer for the stratagems that
> homosexuals in all branches of the theater are now
> often forced to use in order to work. . . . Homo-
> sexual dramatists need the same liberty that hetero-
> sexuals now have. If this is too much for us to con-
> template, then at least let us drop all the cant about
> "homosexual" influence and distortions because we
> are only complaining of the results of our own
> attitudes.

On Being Different

What a pity that the first really popular play about homosexuals was such self-pitying kitsch as *The Boys in the Band*, although maybe the kitsch accounts for its popularity. Maybe some people want to think that's the way homosexuals are, and, of course, some are, none that I have known, though, not for long anyway.

And some homosexuals are like the four wild heterosexuals in *Who's Afraid of Virginia Woolf?* It is best to avoid them. Do you wonder that sometimes for weeks on end I never leave the house?

A few years ago I made some complaint about my current relationship to an old friend, and he said, "But I thought that was a good relationship."

I said, no doubt with an inner sigh, "It is, but it's a relationship."

It has been my observation, and I have done considerable looking into the matter, that relationships are very much the same, no matter what the sex of the people involved. It's never easy. I've tried it three times on what I hoped would be a permanent basis. Once, the marriage; the second affinity lasted ten years, each more tortured than the one before. The third has lasted six years now, and once we got acquainted, which took a little more than two and a half years, it has been beautiful. Except for a slight suspicion, now and again, that he is a better writer than I am.

Nothing I have written has ever come easily. I read and believe Ben Jonson when he says that Shakespeare never blotted a line, and I believe that Mozart composed the overture to *Don Giovanni* while the first-night audience was walking into the theater. But I realized when I was practicing the piano ten and twelve hours a day in Marshalltown that I would never be another Wolfgang Amadeus, and at about sixteen or so, I decided it was either that or nothing. Nothing.

As a writer, I learned early on to make do with the necessity of blotting lines.

But writing the piece for the *Times* was the most difficult writing of any kind ever. First of all, I tried doing it any way but the right way, any way but honestly. The first version was in the third person and was a once-over-lightly sociological history of what had happened since the Stonewall Rebellion in June, 1969, through the gay-in in June, 1970.

As part of the research I attended several meetings of the Gay Activists' Alliance and the Gay Liberation Front. I was fascinated by both, envied both. They are wonderful kids, honest, unafraid, loving, knowing some things, important things that I'm still not sure about. They may have hang-ups, but guilt is not among them. Neither is cowardice. Huey Newton is perfectly right: homosexuals may be the most revolutionary.

I couldn't help thinking, with the required pinch of rue and regret, how different my life would have been if I had been born homosexual in 1950 instead of . . . But that's a tiresome game, and I'm too old to play it.

Besides, writing about the kids in G.A.A. and G.L.F. wasn't what I had been asked to do or wanted to do. No matter what else, I had to tell what it had been like with me, and that I was not prepared to do, could not bring myself to do. Not easily, anyway.

Afterward, lots of people wrote to say how courageous I had been in doing the piece. Well, maybe, but, as you can see, my heroism came after every conceivable attempt to be something less than that, anything less than that.

In late October, when I was still trying to begin the piece, the Gay Activists' Alliance had its all-day sit-in at *Harper's*; I was unable to join in. I did, however, write a note saying to the editors, saying for the first time, that these were my friends, my brothers and sisters. I was homosexual, I said, and while I was not among them, I was with them.

A few days after that the story about E. M. Forster and his posthumous homosexual novel appeared in the *Times*, and the next day I began the piece, liberated somehow, the block unblocked.

I had admired Forster since the day I first happened on *Howard's End*. Admired him both as a writer and as a man:

I believe in aristocracy. . . . Not an aristocracy of power, based upon rank and influence, but an aristocracy of the sensitive, the considerate, and the plucky. Its members are to be found in all nations and classes, and through all the ages, and there is a secret understanding between them when they meet. They represent the true human tradition, the one queer victory of our race over cruelty and chaos.

(I had, with Forster's permission, used *A Secret Understanding* as the title of a novel, along with that quotation from his essay "What I Believe.")

I wrote the article in six days, against the advice of every friend I had or have, homosexual and straight. I lost a couple even before it was published, both homosexuals of my generation, ". . . of course I won't be able to see you again if you write something like that . . . and of *all* places to advertise, the *Times*."

More usual were people who said, who always say, "Well, if you do it, I hope you're prepared for the consequences." Nobody added, as my mother invariably did after issuing that particular ultimatum, "And, afterward, don't come home, your tail between your legs, crying to me . . ."

A friend who read the article just before I sent it to the *Times* said, "I think it's wonderful, but couldn't you take out that part about the black boys at the M. & St. L. railroad station?"

The *Times* had no objection at all, not to anything; all of the cuts were for reasons of space.

Among the more than two thousand letters I've received since the piece have been a great many saying that having written it, I must surely feel relieved, feel freer somehow; it was all out in the open at last.

But that's like asking whether I regret having written it. I'm not sure whether I feel more free. I may simply feel more naked than before, somehow more exposed, more vulnerable. And again it will be some time before I know for sure, if I ever know for sure.

A fellow writer said on national television, "I don't think a writer should reveal that much of himself."

I have always thought that one of the obligations of a writer is to expose as much of himself as possible, to be as open and honest as he can manage—among other reasons so that his readers can see in what he writes a reflection of themselves, weaknesses and strengths, courage and cowardice, good and evil. Isn't that one of the reasons writing is perhaps the most painful of the arts?

Maybe he's right, though. Maybe I exposed too much of myself. I was told that a woman in Brewster whom I had thought of as a friend had said, rather snappishly, "I think he should have kept a thing like that to himself."

I have lived near the village of Brewster for twenty years now, and it is small; I have a nodding acquaintance with almost everybody. Going there for the first time after the piece appeared was as difficult as—oh, or so my memory insists, making the first island landing in the Pacific in the spring of 1945.

I knew that while by no means everybody in town would have read the article, everybody would either have heard about it or seen or heard about the Cavett Show. Indeed, the day after the show a neighbor to whom I have not been introduced wrote: "I've seen you flitting down the streets of Brewster, and if you continue to write such degenerate . . . and say such filthy . . ."

I would not consider myself a flitter; still, the eye of the beholder . . . A friend had telephoned to say, "There's been a lot of talk around town, and it wouldn't surprise me if the next time you go to the A&P, you are stoned."

Who but a friend would tell you a thing like that?

All right. I know it's ridiculous, but it's true. For three weeks I did not go to Brewster; when I shopped, I went to Danbury, where I am not known.

But one morning my sense of the ridiculous—I like to think it was that—took over, and I allowed myself to be driven (I am one of the non-driving minority) to the village. I went boldly into the stationery store and, feeling like a man attending his own execution, picked up a magazine.

The proprietor of the store came over, smiled, and said, "I want to shake your hand. That was a very important piece you wrote, and I'm glad you did it.

We need to get these things out in the open and discuss them."

So much for the small and shameful fears. Later
that day I talked on the telephone to one of the early
astronauts, a pleasant enough man but one I had
always considered the squarest of the square. Toward
the end of our conversation he said, "I read your piece
in the *Times*. . . . It was very good, very important,
very necessary."

I keep forgetting, and I mustn't, the basic decency
of most people. To repeat, given a chance, most people are basically decent. The young. Oh, yes, the
young; I have always thought that. I have never been
one of those who are threatened by the young. The
girl who was editor of *The Daily Iowan* this year
wrote:

> . . . Articles such as yours make it easier for all
> persons who deviate from the so-called norm (read
> white, straight, middle-class, Protestant male).
> . . . I want to assure you that *The Daily Iowan*
> has (naturally) changed quite a lot since you
> worked for the paper. . . . We have ascribed to the
> principle that all people deserve to have a sense of
> dignity, a sense of worth; that people deserve to be
> judged as human beings above all else. . . . We

understand that all oppression is interrelated: that the treatment accorded blacks, women, gay people, all derives from the same source, that until we are all free, none will be free. . . . I think you would have felt more comfortable working for this year's staff, but we still have a long way to go. We are, however, trying to go the distance.

The young. And sometimes the aging as well. A woman I went to high school with:

. . . Twenty-three and a half years living in the same house, married to the same man and raising five children have made my life one of great happiness rather than unexciting monotony, as it might seem. . . . Everyone is misjudged and misunderstood on occasion, but the shame of our society that we should tolerate discrimination against homosexuals is deplorable, and I cringe to realize I've been even a small part of it! . . . Though I've read much on the subject, from various sources, nothing else has so effectively influenced me. I feel confident that others are gaining a healthier attitude toward this long-existing problem and, hopefully, the present generation will prove wiser than its often closed-minded and narrow-thinking elders.

I am much more optimistic than when I wrote the piece, much; the laws, as I said, will be changed, sooner than I thought. Efforts are under way in every state, and they will, I think, succeed.

I spoke of liberal guilt about homosexuality and said that there was none. As if I thought that guilt was a requisite for doing what is right. And that, of course, is nonsense. I think social attitudes will change, are changing, quickly, too.

Possible parental attitudes as well. True, the principal of an elementary school near New York City wrote that parents would rather hear that their children are mentally retarded or disturbed than hear any mention of homosexuality. On the other hand, a suburban housewife wrote:

A few days after I read Merle Miller's article . . . my husband and I began discussing homosexuality in terms of our two young sons, aged two and a half and seven months. My husband asked how I would react if one of our sons showed a preference for his own sex.

. . . I think I would try to get him to talk about his feelings and then urge him to try psychiatric counseling. (I am supposing that this is occurring when he is in his teens). What started as an experiment could have become a habit rather than a matter of preference.

But thinking of my son as an adult homosexual fills me with neither disgust nor maternal glee that no other woman will take my place, but concern for his fulfillment and happiness. Human beings need to give and receive love. Does it really matter whom we choose to love so long as we are loving?

There was considerable objection among young gays to my statement that, given a choice, I would rather have been straight. The assumption seems to have been that I consider straightness more virtuous, somehow superior. That was not what I meant. I meant that in this place and this time, indeed in most others since the Hellenic Age in Greece, being straight is easier. But as the son of a novelist wrote:

. . . the point has to be made—and I think your article remains ambiguous on this—that it's not *being* gay . . . it's having been gay at the time we were, and, especially, it's having been gay in secret, having had a sex life either throttled or separate from our everyday work life, having lived in a world of momentary, anonymous contacts, etc. . . .

None of this is necessary. And all around me now in gay liberation I see people only five to ten years younger than myself (I am twenty-nine), some of them indeed people with several years of heterosexual life behind them, coming out with no guilt at all so far as I can see. For you, "Gay is good. Gay is proud. Well, yes, I suppose." For them it is, period. As a result, your article—totally honest for you—was not totally true for us. This isn't a put-down; it's to say that from where we stand, some things are clear in our lives that can't be part of your experience. For us this was not "what it means to be a homosexual," but what it no longer need mean.

Dozens of letters explained why if they came out of the closet homosexual doctors and therapists would lose their patients, lawyers wrote that they would lose their practices; writers would lose their readers; a producer would not be able to raise the money for his next musical if . . .

Each homosexual must, of course, come out at his own time and in his own way, but homosexuals, the older as well as the younger, the ones in Brooks Brothers suits as well as those in black turtleneck sweaters have, I think, an obligation to declare themselves whenever they decently can.

A boy in Pittsburgh got my telephone number from a mutual acquaintance, and he called to announce that unless he was persuaded to the contrary, he was going to commit suicide. He had been the victim of shameful treatment from the Pittsburgh police department, in particular from a member of the vice squad, whose 219th vice arrest the boy was. And he had got kicked out of the nursing school he was attending, without a hearing.

I advised against the suicide, pointing out that he would miss the gay revolution, and revolutions are always exciting, especially if they are bloodless.

But when I suggested that he go to the Pittsburgh branch of the American Civil Liberties Union and to the local homophile organization for help, he said, "I couldn't do that. If I did, my mother might hear about it, and if she did, it would kill her."

I told him that in general mothers turn out to be sturdier than you think and that they had been hearing such information about their sons for several thousand years now, and I knew of no recorded instance of one dying from the shock.

I think that the boy was convinced that suicide would be a mistake, but I don't think I convinced him that his mother was strong enough to bear the shock. I wanted to tell him that his mother no doubt already knew. The things we spend our lives knowing and pretending not to know . . . I didn't, though; I wished him luck, knowing he'd need it.

63

Not long before last fall's election, a member of the Gay Activists' Alliance told one of Arthur Goldberg's aides that he was grateful for Goldberg's stand on homosexual issues, but added, "Why didn't he do it before?"

"He wasn't asked before," said the aide.

No minority in this country or anywhere else has gained its rights by remaining silent, and no revolution has ever been made by the wary. Or the self-pitying.

I wrote that ". . . the closets are far from emptied; there are more in hiding than out of hiding," and the mail abundantly demonstrates that. It took me a long time to do it, but now that I have, I realize how stifling the air has been all these years. I may not be freer, but I'm a lot more comfortable, a lot less cramped.

And there are smaller pleasures involved. I for one will never again have to listen to and pretend to laugh at the latest "fag gag"; I will never again have to describe the airline stewardess who had the hots for me ". . . and so when we got to Chicago, we went to the hotel, and . . ." I will never again have to shake my head when some insensitive, malicious boob says, "Of course, I've never *known* any fags, have you? I

mean, except this one fag hairdresser who is always
. . ."

Never ever again.

I now go along with James Blake, the author of a
marvelous book about, among other things, prison
life; he is Genet with a sense of humor. He wrote:

> I've been homosexual (stupid term) for a long
> time, and I was never much bothered by what
> people thought, though I always kept a wary eye
> on the fuzz. . . . It was never a problem with me—
> I figured the kind of people who take exception to
> my sex life are people I don't want to know any-
> way. So no sweat.

Why was I always bothered?

About the Author

MERLE MILLER grew up in Marshalltown, Iowa, and attended the Universities of Iowa and London. He has been an editor at *Harper's,* and still writes frequently for that magazine, *Esquire* and others. Among his published works are *That Winter,* a novel, and *Only You, Dick Darling!,* a best-selling nonfiction account of his experiences in the world of television. Mr. Miller is also the author of a new novel, to be published in the spring of 1972.